D.A.R.E.

(Doing All Required and Expecting)

TO

SUCCEED

AND

PROSPER

Apostle Bennie Fluellen

Dare to Succeed and Prosper

Copyright © 1998 by Bennie Fluellen.

All rights reserved. No part of this book may be reproduced or transmitted in any form or by any means without written permission from the author.

ISBN: 0-9671194-0-5
First Printing, 1998
Second Printing, 2000
Third Printing 2013
Printed in USA

Dedication

First, I want to thank God for His trust in me. He has called me to an awesome and great responsibility. He brought me through periods of life that have prepared me for this particular assignment.

I want to thank God for the foundation of family that includes first and foremost a wonderful, loving, and supportive wife, Delores Fluellen. Words cannot adequately express my deep love and appreciation for my partner in life. I love you and thank God for you. I also thank my daughter, Anitra, who worked with me on this book. What an inspiration you have been to my life and I look forward to seeing your success and prosperity exceeding that of my own.

To my wonderful church family, Overflow Ministries Covenant Church, Inc. What a privilege it has been to pastor you and share with you what God has shared with me. I look forward to all the success stories that shall flow out of Overflow Ministries. God has called us to be both successful and prosperous. To my Pastor of 18 years, spiritual mentor, beloved cousin and brother, Bishop Michael Dantley, thank you for the years of experience and allowing me to build confidence in what God has called me to be and do. Many thanks for the opportunities to succeed and prosper in my home church, Christ Emmanuel Christian Fellowship.

To my very good friends, covenant brothers and co-laborers in ministry, whose friendships and relationships contributed to the completion of this work: Prophet Kevin Leal, Bishop Carl C. Alexander, Apostle Barry Chaney, Prophet Lynn Hiles, Bishop David Huskins, and Pastor Marlon Reid. You will never know how much you mean to me and how much you are part of the writing of this book. A word of thanks to Elder Monica Keenon for all your hard work to make this possible. It has been a pleasure to work with you. Not only is it a pleasure, but an honor because we create well together and you bring out the creativity within me. Thanks for many long hours of editing and brainstorming to make this book a reality. Thanks to Elder Rose Durham for your typing and other assistance in this project.

Finally, but certainly not least, I thank God for my biological parents Bennie (Ben) Fluellen, Sr. and Ruby Edwards Wright who are now both deceased. You were the conduits for my entrance into this world to start and finish my course; to the woman who raised me and essentially the only mother I have ever known – Mattie Fluellen, I love you and thank you for doing your part in my destiny. I love you all.

A very special thank you to the following for their seed sown into this project: Donald and Auelia Adams,

Dare To Succeed and Prosper

Phillip and Danielle Baker, Reggie and Sharon Crowell, Elders Paul and Rose Durham, Larry and Jackie Floyd, James and Yvette Foster, Deacons Buck and Catanna Gibson, Carolyn Haines, Elder Monica Keenon, Carl McCrary, Gary and Delores Overstreet, John and Nyria Pearl, William and Julia Pitts, Deonne Rhodes, Papa Joe and Mother Gwen Steward, Franco Tillman, Valerie Dawson, Mom Tolbe, Nathan Wilks, Danita Woods, Bert and Phyllis Williams, Linda Scott and Roger Zellars.

May the Lord cause you to abound more and more; and may the God of increase make you overflow in all things pertaining to life and Godliness.

CONTENTS

	Foreword	Page 7
1	I Dare You	Page 13
2	What Are You Afraid Of	Page 19
3	Zealous For The Good Life	Page 26
4	Your Mind Matters	Page 31
5	Picturing Success	Page 37
6	Good Success…God's Desire	Page 45
7	Framing Your World For Success	Page 53
8	Successful Meditations	Page 63
9	Praying For Success	Page 70
10	What's Missing?	Page 76
11	It's Not a Sin to Prosper	Page 81
12	Creating an Overflow	Page 87

Foreword
By Prophet Lynn Hiles

In an hour when men's hearts are failing them for fear, it is encouraging to find a piece of literature that can address with straightforward practical instruction, steps that can be taken to remove from Christians, the crippling effect that years of erroneous teachings have produced in their thinking. We have often been taught a losing mentality. Losing mentalities many times are preached by the majority, as was the case with the children of Israel when they sent spies into the land of promise. Ten of them came back with a message declaring how big Giants were, and how thick the walls were and all the reasons why they could not take what God said was theirs.

However, in the mouth of a minority, two spies had a different message with a completely different focus; a report based on the promises of God and the Word of the Lord. They were not foolishly reaching for some far-fetched idea hoping it would pan out. They were moving by faith, which was a product of hearing the Word of the Lord. They were not listening to the crippling words of those that were telling them that they were grasshoppers in their own eyes, and therefore they were grasshoppers to their enemies. What the crawling locust left, the swarming locust has eaten, and what the swarming locust left, the hopping locust has eaten; and what the hopping locust left, the stripping locust has eaten (Joel 1:4). In this text, Joel is prophesying of an army that has devastated the Garden of God and left a tremendous famine and a deficit of corn, wine, and oil.

I don't believe that in our day, they are literal armies that are marching, but they are a parade of losing mentalities, grasshopper mentalities that begin crawling, and then progressively swarming, then hopping and ultimately stripping and leaving us weak and powerless people that cannot fulfill their destinies.

However, John the Baptist in Matthew 3 came eating locust. The man was a bug eater. In other words, he had a ministry that destroyed losing mentalities. Moreover, that message was repent, from the Greek word metanoeo which means to think differently. This book, so masterfully written, does exactly that. It challenges you to repent and think differently for the Kingdom of God is at hand, it is within your reach. Whose report will you believe? I trust that you will believe the report of the Lord that comes from Pastor Fluellen as he challenges you to take your promised land.

Dare To Succeed and Prosper

WHAT'S MISSING?

S _ CCESS

Apostle Bennie Fluellen

Successful people are dreamers

who have found a dream too exciting, too important to remain in the realm of fantasy.

And, who day by day, hour by hour,

toil in the service of their dream, until they can touch it with their hands and see it with their eyes.

(Earl Nightingale)

I

DARE

YOU!

Apostle Bennie Fluellen

Joshua 1:5-9

"There shall not any man be able to stand before thee all the days of thy life; as I was with Moses, so I will be with thee: I will not fail thee, nor forsake thee. Be strong and of a good courage; for unto this people shalt thou divide for an inheritance the land, which I sware unto their fathers to give them. Only be thou strong and very courageous, that thou mayest observe to do according to all the law, which Moses my servant commanded thee: turn not from it to the right hand or to the left, that thou mayest prosper withersoever thou goest. This book of the law shall not depart out of thou mouth; but thou shalt meditate therein day and night, that thou mayest observe to do according to all that is written therein: for then thou shalt make thy way prosperous, and then thou shalt have good success. Have not I commanded thee? Be strong and of a good courage; be not afraid, neither be thou dismayed: for the Lord thy God is with thee withersoever thy goest."

CHAPTER

1

I DARE YOU!

> **DARE** - to have the courage required for; to challenge someone; to do something requiring boldness.

As God's creation, we must remember that dominion is not just our right, but it is our responsibility. Genesis 1:26-28

> *"And God said, Let us make man in our image,*
>
> *and after our likeness and let them have*
>
> *DOMINION over the fish of the sea, and over*
>
> *the fowl of the air, and over the cattle and*

over every creeping thing that creepeth upon the earth. So God created man in his own image, in the image of God created He him, male and female created He them. And God blessed them, and God said unto them, Be fruitful and multiply and replenish the earth and subdue it; and have DOMINION over the fish of the sea, and over the fowl of the air, and over every living thing that moveth upon the earth."

This particular passage of scripture gives us the genesis or the beginning of God's design and will for mankind. We were designed for dominion! We were made to have aurthority and to be God's earthly agents over all of His creation. David even got a revelation of this wondrous responsibility when he penned the words in Psalm 8:4-8

"What is man that thou art mindful of him? and the son of man, that thou visitest him? for thou hast made him a little lower than the angels, and hast crowned him with glory and honour. Thou madest him to have

dominion over the works of thy hands; thou hast put all things under his feet: All sheep and oxen, yea, and the beasts of the field; the fowl of the air, and the fish of the sea, and whatsoever passeth though the paths of the sea."

For years, I believe that we have been made to believe only a portion of the Gospel – The Good News. The Good News is not just that God sent His Son in the likeness of sinful flesh to condemn sin in the flesh and to deliver us from our sins. But God sent His Son to save everything that was lost during the fall.

Since the fall of Adam brought about dispossession in terms of our position in the earth realm, it now becomes necessary for the Believer to be restored and to have dominion. The god of this world is trying to make us believe that he is the heir apparent to the earth. But not so! As the rightful heirs of the earth, we must take our rightful positions as priests and kings in the earth. In taking our rightful places, the god of this world will oppose the Kingdom of God. But we have our instructions of how we deal with such opposition through the Word of God in **Matthew 11:12.**

Apostle Bennie Fluellen

"The Kingdom of God suffereth violence, but the violent taketh by force."

As born-again Christians filled with God's Spirit and Presence, this world ought to know that we are a force to be reckoned with! Filled with God's Spirit and His Presence we are guaranteed to succeed. However great this guarantee or promise, we still seem to lack the courage to move forward.

Since early on in history, challenges have been made to God's people; and the majority of them have remained couched in their cowardice state, filled with fear. Such was the case of the army of Israel prior to the heroic story of David and Goliath as we know it.

"The Philistines stood on a mountain on one side, and Israel stood on a mountain on the other side, with a valley between them. And a champion went out from the camp of the Philistines, named Goliath from Gath, whose height was six cubits and a span. He had a bronze helmet on his head, and he was armed with a coat of mail, and the weight of the coat was five thousand shekels of bronze. And he had bronze armor on his legs and a bronze javelin between his shoulders. Now the staff of his spear was like a weaver's beam, and his iron spearhead weighed six hundred shekels; and a shield bearer went before him. Then he stood and cried out to

the armies of Israel, and said to them, "Why have you come out to line up for battle? Am I not a Philistine, and you the servants of Saul? Choose a man for yourselves and let him come down to me. If he is able to fight with me and kill me, then we will be your servants, But if I prevail against him and kill him, then you shall be our servants and serve us." And the Philistine said, "I defy the armies of Israel this day; give me a man, that we may fight together." When Saul and all Israel heard these words of the Philistine, they were dismayed and greatly afraid." **1 Samuel 17:1-8**

Goliath challenged all of Israel. He issued a DARE, and what did God's people do including the leader? They did NOTHING! Their emotional response was that of **dismay** and **fear.** In being dismayed, they lost heart and courage. The emotional state of dismay will produce other negative or disempowering emotions and attitudes.

> **"ALL SERIOUS DARING STARTS FROM WITHIN."**
>
> *Eudora Welty*

One such attitude systemic of dismay is fear. Fear is debilitating! It is paralyzing! It will always keep you from making decisions that empower you. Nobody wanted to step forward and accept the challenge.

Do you remember growing up as a child and having neighborhood or school bullies who would always challenge and intimidate others? If so, you will recall that the bully's reign of terror increased, until someone stepped up to the plate and accepted their challenge. When a bully is left unchallenged, he or she doesn't stop until they find someone who is bold enough to say, "I'm not afraid of you!"

David, now empowered by his decision to stand toe to toe with the giant, is left with the consequence of enacting his courageous decision. A bully's reign is immediately threatened once someone finally finds the courage to stand up and not back down.

CHAPTER 2

What Are You Afraid Of?

> "THE ONLY THING WE HAVE TO FEAR IS FEAR ITSELF."
>
> *President Franklin D. Roosevelt*

Are you afraid of success and prosperity or are you afraid of failure? Whichever might be the case, it is that fear that is keeping you from becoming the successful and prosperous person that God intended. There are two particular quotes that I would like to reference at this point to further clarify my point regarding fear of failure.

"You cannot discover new oceans unless you have

the courage to lose sight of the shore."

Another quote is like it.

"The fishermen know that the sea is terrible, but they

have never found these dangers sufficient reason

for remaining ashore."

FEAR OF SUCCESS IS EQUALLY AS POWERFUL AS FEAR OF FAILURE!

Success demands that you get rid of fear. One cannot be successful while embracing fear. Successful people are people who respond to challenges with assurance and belief. There are people who are not afraid of failure but, they are afraid of success. Some people have become so accustomed to a life of mediocrity, that they are afraid of the challenges that success brings. Don't be afraid of failure. Don't be afraid of success. Boldly declare that fear can no longer dictate your steps and you will release unlimited potential that will propel you towards the journey of Success and Prosperity.

Fear is empowered when we constantly refuse to meet our challenges and/or circumstances head on. We are admonished over and over again in God's word not to fear.

Deut. 31:8

"And the Lord, He it is that doth go before thee; He will be with thee, He will not fail thee, neither forsake thee: FEAR NOT, NEITHER BE DISMAYED."

Psalm 27:1

"The Lord is my light and my salvation; whom shall I fear? The Lord is the strength of my life; of whom shall I be afraid?"

Isaiah 41:10

"Fear thou not; for I am with thee: be not dismayed; for I am thy God: I will strengthen thee; yea, I will help thee; yea, I will uphold thee with the right hand of My righteousness."

Romans 8:15(a)

"For ye have not received the spirit of bondage again to fear;..."

2 Timothy 1:7

"For God hath not given us the spirit of fear; but of power, and of love, and of a sound mind."

One of the greatest deterrents to SUCCESS and PROSPERITY is .... FEAR!

FEAR is False Evidence Appearing Real!

In Matthew 25 where we read about the parable of the talents, we find that Jesus rewarded those persons who were industrious and invested their talents and gained more. The servants with the five and two talents respectively, were considered faithful, while the servant who held on to his one talent was considered wicked and lazy. Let's look at the master's response to the wicked servant.

Matthew 25:24-27

"Then he which had received the one talent came and said, lord, I knew thee that thou art an hard man, reaping where thou hast not sown, and gathering where thou hast not strawed: And I was afraid, and went and hid thy talent in the earth: lo, there thou hast that is thine. His lord answered and said unto him, thou wicked and slothful servant, thou knewest that I reap where I sowed not, and gathered where I have not strawed: Thou

oughtest therefore to have put my money to the exchangers, and then at my coming I should have received mine own with usury (interest)."

This servant was considered wicked and slothful. Notice that it was his fear that kept him from stepping out and doing something with what he had been given. He said, "…I was afraid, and went and hid thy talent in the earth."

Fear is akin to LAZINESS!

In Joshua 1, we immediately see that after God proclaimed his promises to Joshua he gets specific instructions to be strong and courageous. Not only are these instructions specific, but they are repeated in verses 6, 7, and 9.

Joshua 1:6

"Be strong and of good courage......"

Joshua 1:7

"Only be thou strong and very courageous...."

Joshua 1:9

"Have I not commanded thee? Be strong and of a

good courage; be not afraid, neither be thou dismayed..."

It is important to note that verses 6 and 7 are descriptive in nature. In other words, Joshua was to be strong and courageous. But verse 9 depicts a mindset of knowing that God is with him.

"Be strong and of a good courage; be not afraid, neither be thou dismayed: for the Lord thy God is with thee whithersoever thou goest."

It is important for us to know that the people of God were not intimidated for a brief period of time, but 1 Samuel 17:16 points out that the giant, Goliath challenged and dared them for forty days from morning to evening. As David was taking food to his brethren involved in the battle, Goliath repeated his challenge to them yet another time. But this time, it was in the presence of David.

The men of Israel fled because of their continued fear of Goliath's challenge (See Verse 25). The very interesting thing is that there was a great reward offered for the man who would stand up and fight victoriously against this giant. The man who would accept this challenge would be honored with great riches, have the king's daughter as his wife, and exempt the man's entire family from taxes in Israel. What a reward! But still no challengers; how sad!

As is the custom for anyone who wouldn't **DARE to**

SUCCEED and PROSPER, David's brother viewed his willingness to step out and do what he wouldn't do as pride and arrogance. Oftentimes, fearful and fretful individuals mistake boldness as pride and arrogance.

Boldness ought to be a characteristic possessed and nurtured by all of those who call themselves to be Christ's very own. For He is the Lion of the Tribe of Judah and He is alive within us. Therefore, BOLDNESS is an appropriate attribute for the believer.

"...the [uncompromisingly] righteous are as bold as a lion." **Proverbs 28:1 (AMP)**

CHAPTER 3

Zealous For The Good Life

> **ZEAL** - Enthusiastic and diligent devotion as to a cause.

Zeal is essential for one to succeed and prosper. Unfortunately, zeal has taken on a negative image in the Christian community as we have referenced the scripture concerning the people's zeal that was not according to knowledge. However, an enthusiastic and diligent approach to a cause is essential to success and prosperity.

Zealousness is birthed out of boldness. Any person zealous to do something always exhibit boldness! Prior to the Apostle Paul's conversion he was noted for his zealousness in persecuting the saints.

Philippians 3:6 (AMP)

"As to my zeal, I was a persecutor of the church, and by the Law's standard of righteousness supposed justice, uprightness, and right standing with God) I was proven to be blameless and no fault was found with me."

Paul's zealousness to persecute the Church was birthed out of his boldness concerning what he believed to be truth. Now having come into the light of the Glorious Gospel of Jesus Christ who is the Truth; he doesn't ignore zeal, he simply redirects it. Therefore, Paul encourages us in Romans 12:11 that we should be zealous.

Romans 12:11 (AMP)

"Never lag in zeal and in earnest endeavor; be aglow and burning with the Spirit, serving the Lord."

We love to talk about the fact that Christ has come to redeem us from the curse and how he has chosen us as His own, special people. In Titus 2:14 we understand that there is more to why He has redeemed and chosen us.

Titus 2:14

"Who gave Himself for us, that he might redeem us from all iniquity, and purify unto Himself a peculiar people, ZEALOUS of good works."

The Amplified version renders it this way:

"Who gave Himself on our behalf that He might redeem us (purchase our freedom) from all iniquity and purify for Himself a people [to be peculiarly his own, people who are] eager and enthusiastic about [living a life that is good and filled with] beneficial deeds."

As God's people, we should be zealous towards our motivations and goals.

This is what I believe David meant when he said in

1 Samuel 17:29, *"... is there not a cause?"* When there is a cause that you believe in it will inevitably motivate or thrust you into action.

One can always dream and desire success and prosperity. But when zeal is absent, it simply becomes hope. It is not enough to simply hope for something. Zeal moves you into action. Without action supporting your dreams and desires, one can become discouraged and frustrated. This hinders or delays that for which we hope.

"Hope deferred maketh the heart sick: but when the desire cometh, it is a tree of life."

I BELIEVE I CAN FLY

(Lyrics written and recorded by R. Kelley)

I used to think that I could not go on

And life was nothing but an awful song;

but now I know the meaning of true love

I'm leaning on the everlasting arms;

If I can see it then I can do it

If I just believe it, there's nothing to it.

I BELIEVE I can fly,

I BELIEVE I can touch the sky;

I think about it every night and day

Spread my wings and fly away;

I BELIEVE I can soar,

I see me running through that open door

I BELIEVE I can fly,

Apostle Bennie Fluellen

I BELIEVE I can fly,

I BELIEVE I can fly

See I was on the verge of breaking down

Sometimes silence can seem to be so loud.

There are miracles in life I must achieve;

But first I know it starts inside of me

If I can see it, then I can be it;

I I just BELIEVE it, there's nothing to it.

I BELIEVE I can fly

I BELIEVE I can touch the sky

I think about it every night and day;

Spread my wings and fly away,

I BELIEVE I can soar,

I See me running through that open door

I BELIEVE I can fly

I BELIEVE I can fly

I BELIEVE I can fly...

Cause I BELIEVE in me, Cause I BELIEVE in you!

CHAPTER 4

Your Mind Matters

For some strange reason, the average Christian has been told that since he/she is now born again, the mind can now be disengaged. And for the Christian, who is filled with the Holy Ghost or baptized in the Holy Ghost, he/she has been deceived into thinking that *(because of the Holy Ghost's powerful presence in you),* the use of the mind is unnecessary. We are thereby robbed of maintaining not merely a successful life, but the life that Christ came to give us.

John 10:10

"The thief does not come except to steal, and to kill, and to destroy. I have come that they may have life,

and that they may have it more abundantly."

This abundant life is an OVERFLOWING LIFE . This is God's prosperity! God's covenant with his people is not "not enough" or "just enough" ... but more than enough! In the beginning God placed us in a finished work in the Garden of Eden where he declared everything to be good. The earth was then handed over to man and he was given dominion over all of it. Not only was he given dominion over it all; but also the universal command to reproduce, be fruitful and multiply. Now this speaks of increase, more than enough, or PROSPERITY. This clearly demonstrates that God's idea from the very beginning was for man to be enriched and to have a prosperous, abundant and overflowing life! From John 10: 10 we see that God's plan for sending Jesus included not only salvation, but also the restoration of all things and to expose the devils' intent to hinder our receiving what God has always intended.

As non-believers, our minds were hindered from the glorious Gospel of Christ. And after coming to Christ, many of us still grope in darkness even though we've been translated into the kingdom of light. Thus Paul says to us:

<u>Romans 12:2</u>

"....and be not conformed to this world, but be ye transformed by the renewing of your mind."

Your Thinking Is Influenced By Things And People!

Therefore, in order to receive all that God has for us, our subconscious minds must be renewed. When we usually talk about the renewing of the mind as Paul discusses in Romans 12, we usually think very generally about the mind never giving thought to how our conscious mind is renewed.

UNDERSTANDING THE MIND

The mind is divided into the conscious and subconscious minds. The conscious mind is the decision-maker. It is here in the consciousness that the question of WHAT? is addressed. The Subconscious mind is the provision maker. It is here in the subconsciousness that the question of HOW is addressed.

The conscious mind of an individual cannot use all the signals, messages, or information that is sent to it. So the brain filters and stores the information it needs or expects to need later, and allows the conscious mind of the individual to ignore the rest.

The subconscious mind has a direct affect on the

condition of the conscious mind. To really know the mind of someone, you cannot be deceived by their conscious mind. But it is only in the subconscious mind that our true state of mind can be discerned. Our true state of mind determines our behavior or actions. It is our 'state of mind' that gives power to our conscious mind. Whether they be empowering or disempowering.

DISEMPOWERING STATES OF MIND:

Fear, Doubt, Anxiety, Sadness, Frustration, Hatred, and Confusion.

These disempowering states of the subconscious mind are paralyzing. They do not engage the conscious mind. These states of mind are the seeds for failure.

EMPOWERING STATES OF MIND:

Courage, Certainty, Joy, Pride (sense of accomplishment) and Love!

Empowering states of mind tap into our real power. For the scripture teaches that as a man thinks in his heart, so is he. **(Prov. 23:7)**

The Thought Life Is Significant To Success!

Empowering states of mind such as Courage, Certainty, Joy, Pride (Sense of Accomplishment) and Love motivates us to agree with God and see what God sees concerning ourselves and our situations. No matter how bleak our current situations may appear, you must view them as false evidence appearing real - F.E.A.R.

One of the most beloved Psalms of all of Christendom is found in Psalm 27. This Psalm speaks of David's confidence in the midst of danger or a deficient situation. Historically this Psalm is divided into two Psalms, the first (vv 1-6) a psalm of confidence and the second (vv 7-14) an individual lament. However in verse 13 it explodes into encouragement and an empowering state of mind when David declared:

> *"I would have fainted (lost heart), unless I had believed to see the goodness of the Lord in the land of the living."*

David did not see what he wanted to see in the natural, he said, "I would have fainted unless I had believed to see"...! What a powerful state of mind! What a powerful use of the imagination! What he believed to see caused him to rise from despair to reign in victory.

SEEING is BELIEVING!

Nelson Mandela, considered one of the present world's greatest leaders, spent 27 years in prison. He is quoted as saying that he constantly visualized himself walking out of the bondages of his prison cell stronger and leading his people to the freedom they so desperately deserved. Today he is hailed as one of the world's greatest leaders. Not because of his charisma, but because of his determination and dream that became a reality. As a result, South Africa will never be the same!

Knowledge Liberates People and Encourages Them To Have The Mind Of God Concerning Possibilities…ALL THINGS ARE POSSIBLE TO THEM THAT BELIEVE!

CHAPTER 5

Picturing Success

(Imagination and Vision)

IMAGINATION - is the process or power of forming a mental image of something that is not or has not been seen or experienced in the physical realm.

Ephesians 3:20

"Now unto Him who is able to do exceeding, abundantly, above all that we could ask, think (or imagine) according to the power that is at work within us."

Success and Prosperity are built upon Vision and Goals.

VISION – is intelligent foresight; a mental image produced by the imagination; something perceived through unusual means as supernatural sight.

Proverbs 29:18

"Where there is no vision, the people perish."

If there is not a redemption revelation, people cast off restraint or have no knowledge of where they're going and what they're doing. To achieve Godly success, you must become a visionary. It is important that we see what God sees. When we see what God sees, and have knowledge of what God knows then are we prime candidates for Success and Prosperity.

If I cannot envision myself being successful and prosperous, then it will not happen.

Vision is being able to see. If you study the Bible you will see that innumerable miracles were performed by Jesus in healing the blind or restoring their sight. Why?

An impaired vision hinders our progress. When our vision is impaired we have to be led from without rather than from within. And when we are led from without, we are at the mercy of those assisting us in seeing and they usually take us where they want to go or where they want us to go, not where we want to go when we want to go!

Knowledge Gets Rid of Your Settling Mentality!

Visualization can act as a prophet in your life. For

visualization is prophesying. Let's see what Habbakuk the prophet has to say.

Habbakuk 2:1-4

"I will stand my watch and set myself on the rampart, and watch to see what He (the Lord) will say to me, and what I will answer when I am corrected. Then the Lord answered me and said: "Write the vision, and make it plain on tablets, that he may run who reads it. For the vision is yet for an appointed time; but at the end it will speak, and it will not lie. Though it tarries, wait for it; Because it will surely come, it will not tarry. Behold the proud, His soul is not upright in him; But the just shall live by his faith."

MY IMAGINATION CREATES MY REALITIES.

Walt Disney

When you visualize something, it clarifies what your desire is. Imagination is creative power. Visualization is putting your thoughts in pictures. We are always motivated by our imaginations. If we are afraid or fearful of doing something, it is because we have imagined that we will fail. We have seen ourselves attempting that thing and failing in our efforts. If we are not afraid, but courageous in attempting something, it is because we have imagined that we will succeed. We have seen ourselves attempting that thing and being successful in our efforts.

Once I have visualized my desire, I need to then write the vision and make it plain. For some, this is considered an action plan or goal setting. Now my vision has become reality in that I have removed it from my mind and brought it into the seen realm. Usually, if we do not write down what we see we become confused by what we think we want and really have nothing to confirm what we thought we saw if it should appear remotely in the tangible realm.

I remember when the Lord spoke to me concerning starting Overflow Ministries. I immediately wrote what I heard the Lord say and what I visualized. This process has helped me greatly, as I look back two years later to see if what I am doing now matches what I originally saw. Even in our local assembly, every prophetic word is transcribed and reviewed often for visualization. It is only after I have written the vision down as a reference point can I determine the degree of my success in accomplishing tasks on my way to success.

One of the most successful persons in the business world

was Walt Disney. It is said that Walt Disney visualized everything before he did them. Whatever he imagined, he visualized. He is quoted as having said, "My imagination creates my realities".

Habbakuk makes it clear that when the vision is written and made plain, he who reads it can pursue it or run after it.

> **Once You Know What You Want, the Resources of TIME, MONEY, AND PEOPLE will show up.**

I will never forget the various experiences that I've had through the years when embarking upon projects. One year I put together a retail clothing store for my wife. Once I had made the decision to do so, I began to see properties that could house the venture. Vendors and suppliers for the merchandise began to find me before we ever opened the store. Upon our decision to open, one concern that I had was the financial resources. But I quickly learned that the decision I made opened various avenues of finance for us. The Lord showed us how to access the financial institutions to acquire the necessary funds to open. Once open, money begot money. Money spent produced more money. People showed up with money and time to help us with our vision.

Another time when I was given the responsibilities at my

home church to manage certain projects from conception to reality, furniture for a restaurant and other parts of the building came when a decision had been made. Interestingly enough, I was able to find and negotiate a deal relative to the project furnishing the entire restaurant and other parts of the building for less than $2,500.

When starting Overflow Ministries, the resources of time, money, and people didn't bother to show up until my decision was made known and acted upon. I can still hear the prophetic words spoken over my life in Chicago, Illinois that God was calling people into this dream with me. In August, 1996 approximately 30 people including children showed up. By November, 1996 an additional 30 people had shown up. And by our first year anniversary more than 100 people had been drawn into the vision. To-date, not even two years from conception, approximately 250 people have shown up with time, money and other resources to fulfill what had been visualized. Another part of the vision for Overflow that I saw was a beautiful non-traditional building utilized to house our ministries and host our celebration services. When you know what you saw, then things that you see along the way will not be able to distract you and keep you from getting what you saw. When you know what to say yes to, saying no is easier because it doesn't look like what you saw. The prophetic word came to me in Kirksville, Missouri through a man who has come to be my very good friend, Kevin Leal. The Word of the Lord came to me saying, "*...**And Son, I want you to build me a house that looks like the finest hotel in that city**....*"

And not even two years into the action steps towards the vision, we were positioned to embark upon a building project from the ground up that would be the physical manifestation of what was produced through words and visualization. While we delayed the building process at that time, today when people walk into our building, the first thing that people say that it looks like a hotel in here. But, none of this would have come to pass had I not **DARE**(d) to do something.

"Understanding Focuses Your Vision." *Kevin Leal*

---

1 Corinthians 2:9-12

"But as it is written: Eye has not seen, nor ear heard, nor have entered into the heart of man the things which God has prepared for those who love Him. But God has revealed them to us through His Spirit. For the Spirit searches all things, yes the deep things of God. For what man knows the things of God except the Spirit of God. Now we have received, not the spirit of the world, but the Spirit who is from God that we might know the things that have been freely given to us by God."

Apostle Bennie Fluellen

If we can only see what God sees! This is not a statement of ability, but rather of believing to see. For no matter what arises against us, we must be certain that:

> *"...If God is for us, who can be against us? He who did not spare His own Son, but delivered Him up for us all, how shall He not with Him also freely give us all things."*

CHAPTER 6

Good Success... God's Desire For You

> **SUCCESS** - the achievement of something desired or attempted; the gaining of fame or prosperity.

Joshua 1:8(b)

"...then thou shall make thy way prosperous and have good success."

The word success in the context of this scripture is from

the Hebrew word sakal. Sakal (succeed) means to be circumspect; to be intelligent; to have insight, to be prudent; to do purposely. Sakal relates to an intelligent knowledge of the reason. In other words, success comes through applying common sense or knowledge.

IN ORDER TO SUCCEED, I MUST KNOW WHAT I MUST DO!

Many Christians do not ascribe to the notion of success because they think that:

(1) Success is tied to money only and money is evil.

(2) Heaven is their reward for earthly sorrow and suffering. Thus any enjoyment on earth (especially success), forfeits their eternal reward of Heaven.

Success does not mean that you worship money. So then, what exactly is biblical success. Before delving into biblical success, let us look at some of the issues surrounding success in an effort to determine success as God defines it for the Believer.

Success is always measured by a set of standards established by some person or group. Therefore, we must ask the following questions in the order presented below.

- ♦ Who Defines Success?
- ♦ Why Do We Pursue Success?
- ♦ What is the Cost of Success?
- ♦ How Do We Pursue Success?

True success is not climbing a ladder, because many who have successfully climbed discovered that the ladder was leaning on the wrong wall. This discovery brings frustration instead of happiness and contentment. To ensure success in every area of our lives requires the adherence to the command found in **Matthew 6:33.**

"But seek ye first the Kingdom of God, and His righteousness; and all these things shall be added unto you."

Many utilize this scripture to oppose success because of the material gain that comes along with it. Properly understood, this text can literally free you from the bonds of poverty and eradicate your "Losing Mentality". A few verses prior to verse 33, we find one of Jesus' discussions regarding treasures.

Much of our distorted mindset regarding success and prosperity stems from the absence of a Kingdom mentality. It is clear that we are to seek first the Kingdom of God. The Kingdom of God is not Heaven. But the Kingdom of God encompasses the Kingdom of Heaven. Heaven is often confused with the Kingdom of God. I firmly believe in the eternal rest of the believer as is traditionally taught. But Heaven must not become our reason for not pursuing success. Heaven is for those who have been born again and for those who have been faithful in their walk with the Lord Jesus Christ. But success is for those who are faithful to pursue their goals and dreams. There is only one way to Heaven --- Jesus Christ; but there are many ways to SUCCESS.

As a citizen of the Kingdom of God, I am governed by Kingdom principles and laws. The idea and notion of family then becomes a major foundation for my life. When God created the family, he had purpose in mind. Created in the image and likeness of God, man and the first family were to have dominion over that which had been created. Success at the price of family is FAILURE personified.

Success in industry, whether it be any type of business venture, professional and/or career achievement is commonly sought after. However, few are those who find it. God is not hiding it from them, but success only comes through faithfulness. As Christians, we love to talk about faith and living by faith. Faith is required in order for the Believer to obtain Godly success. Hebrews and Habbakuk instructs us how the just shall live by faith. *(Habbakuk 2:4 and Hebrews 10:38)* As the pound is currency in England, the yen is currency in Japan, the naira is currency in Nigeria; so faith is the currency in the earth realm. Faith has no redemption value in eternity.

Faith is a commodity to be utilized in time. This is to say that in eternity, there is no need for the exercising of faith because faith produces in time what already exists in eternity.

The faith heroes of Hebrews 11 were successful because they were faithful. Though many died not having experienced the promises, they were nevertheless successful. Why? Because they obeyed God.

> **"OBEDIENCE IS MINIMUM SERVICE TO GOD."** *(Richard G. Briley)*

God alone sets the goal or determines the measure of success for each of us. Obtaining biblical success demands the pursuit of God before the pursuit of success.

In a day and age where Christians are enamored with signs, wonders, and miracles, many would view success also as a miracle. Did you know that success is not a miracle? The reason being, is that a miracle is the suspension of natural laws. Success is a result of following natural laws, which the Bible teaches.

DOING SOMETHING GOOD SUCCESSFULLY IS NOT SUCCESS!

In the context of the aforementioned scripture of Joshua 1:8, Success and Prosperity comes when we apply that which we have the intelligence or insight of. Having insight and intelligence will cause one to act purposely and circumspectly. The first part of this scripture teaches:

> *"This book of the law shall not depart out of thy mouth, but thou shalt meditate therein day and night, that thou mayest observe to do according to all that is written therein....."*

The Word of God is consistent throughout. **Psalm 1:1-3** agrees with Joshua 1:8 and states:

> *"Blessed (happy to be envied) is the man who walks not in the counsel of the ungodly, nor stands in the path of sinners, nor sits in the seat of the scornful; but his delight is in the law of the Lord, and in His law he meditates day and night. He shall be like a tree planted by rivers of water, that brings forth its fruit in its season, whose leaf also shall not*

wither; and whatsoever he does shall prosper."

Meditate in the Hebrew (Hagah) means to murmur; to mutter, to speak, to praise; to whisper. Therefore, as we murmur, mutter, or speak that which God has said, we are then careful to do accordingly. And this is what assures us that in so doing we make our way prosperous and we shall have good success.

Therefore, If I DARE to succeed, I must speak that which God has already said. This creates faith. Faith cometh by hearing, and hearing by the word of God. My words have creative power. As God made the world or framed the world by His Words, we too create and bring into existence things that can be seen but are not made by that which we see.

> *"Through faith we understand that the worlds were framed by the word of God, so that things which are seen were not made by things which do appear."*
>
> **(Hebrews 11:3)**

SUCCESS IS NOT A DESTINATION, BUT A JOURNEY!

Paul, the Apostle, gives us some very important information in Romans 12 which many Christians quote, but few of us have attained its revelation and significance. That is, *"....and be not conformed to this world, but be ye transformed by the renewing of your mind."*

CHAPTER 7

Framing Your World For Success

"Now faith is the substance of things hoped for, the evidence of things not seen. For by it the elders obtained a good report. <u>Through faith we understand that the worlds were framed by the word of God</u>, so that things which are seen were not made of things which do appear." **Hebrews 11:1-3**

Words are extremely powerful. Too little attention is given to what comes forth out of our mouths. David, a man after God's own heart, knew the power of his own words.

Psalm 19:14

"Let the words of my mouth, and the meditation of my heart, be acceptable in Thy sight, O Lord, my strength and my Redeemer."

Jesus too, knew the importance of the spoken word.

Matthew 12:34-37

"... for out of the abundance of the heart the mouth speaketh. A good man out of the good treasures of the heart bringeth forth good things; and an evil man out of the evil treasure bringeth forth evil things. But I say unto, that every idle word that men shall speak, they shall give account thereof in the day of judgment. For by thy words thou shalt be justified, and by thy words thou shalt be condemned."

Words create! It was the spoken word that brought creation forth in Genesis. When bringing forth everything out of nothing, it was God's spoken word that He used to bring order back to this earth.

Gen. 1:3 – *And God said, Let there be light: and there was light.*

Gen. 1:6 – *And God said, Let there be a firmament in the midst of the waters, and let it divide the waters from the waters.*

Gen. 1:9 – *And God said, Let the waters under the heaven be gathered together unto one place, and let the dry land appear: and it was so.*

Gen. 1:11 – *And God said, Let the earth bring forth grass, the herb yielding seed, and the fruit tree yielding fruit after its kind, whose seed is in itself, upon the earth:*

Gen. 1:14-15 – *And God said, Let there be lights in the firmament of the heaven to divide the day from the night; and let them be for signs, and for seasons, and for days, and years. And let them be for lights in the firmament of the heaven to give light upon the earth: and it was so.*

Gen. 1:20 – *And God said, Let the waters bring forth abundantly the moving creature that hath life, and fowl that may fly above the earth in the open firmament of heaven.*

Gen. 1:22 – *And God blessed them, saying, Be fruitful, and multiply, and fill the waters in the seas, and let fowl multiply in the earth.*

Gen. 1:24 – *And God said, Let the earth bring forth the living creature after its kind, cattle, and creeping thing, and beast of the earth after its kind: and it was so.*

Gen. 1:26 – *And God said, Let Us make man in Our image, after Our likeness: and let them have dominion over the fish of the sea, and over the fowl of the air, and over the cattle, and over all the earth, and over every creeping thing that creepeth upon the earth.*

Gen. 1:28 – *And God blessed them,* **and God said** *unto them, Be fruitful, and multiply, and replenish the earth, and subdue it: and have dominion over the fish of the sea, and over the fowl of the air, and over every living thing that moveth upon the earth.*

Thus, the scripture says that by faith we understand that the worlds were framed by the spoken Word of God. He created everything with words. He framed the worlds with words.

What an awesome world he framed! Just look around. Now, I ask you, "What are your words framing?" Hopefully, they are creating the visible from the invisible. If you are not creating, then you are destroying. Which do you prefer? Creation or Destruction? If creating is your preference ….. **BELIEVE IT! SAY IT!** Speaking what we believe is faith.

Success and Prosperity like everything else must be done in faith. For that which is not done in faith is sin. (Romans 14:23)

We all say we have faith. When it comes to Success and Prosperity, where is your faith? David's faith in God was exhibited when he answered Goliath's challenge with words and action.

James 2:14;17-18

"What doth it profit, my brethren, though a man say he hath faith, and have not works? Can faith save him?"... "Even so faith, if it hath not works, is dead, being alone."

We really must say what we believe and believe what we say. Did you know that your words demonstrate your belief. We really do not speak or say that which we have not already believed.

Psalm 116:10

"I have believed therefore I have spoken ..."

You speak what you believe. Have you ever wondered why God hates gossip and negative murmuring? Gossip, tail bearing and the likes are powerful. Words do hurt! You see, we do not talk about something or repeat something that we really do not believe. Making it clear

... If "Bro. Door" tells you that "Pastor Shepherd" doesn't like you, then unless you believe that in your heart, you will not repeat it to "Sis. Window" or any other person. You see, before "Bro. Door" told you this thing about "Pastor Shepherd", he too had to believe it was true. Again, you can create or destroy with your words. Belief starts in the heart.

Romans 10:10(a)

"For with the heart man believeth ..."

And once my heart believes, my mouth speaks!

Romans 10:10(b)

"...And with the mouth confession is made unto salvation."

I believe that it is God's desire for me to succeed and prosper. Therefore, my heart instructs my mouth to speak.

Proverbs 16:23

"The heart of the wise teacheth his mouth..."

Having faith for Success and Prosperity will move my mouth. This is faith.

PRAYING IS SAYING!

Mark 11:22-24

*"...Have faith in God. For verily I say unto you, that whatsoever shall **say** unto this mountain, Be thou removed, and be thou cast into the sea; and shall not doubt in his heart, but shall believe that those things which he **saith** shall come to pass; he shall have whatsoever he **saith**. Therefore I say unto you, what things soever ye desire when ye pray, believe that ye receive them, and ye shall have them."*

SAY WHAT YOU BELIEVE ...
THEN BELIEVE WHAT YOU SAY!

We are often told of Daniel's prayer life. We have read and heard of Daniel's prayer in Daniel 9:3-19. In Chapter 10, we find a very interesting scripture containing details that are often overlooked. We know that there was a struggle between the Prince of Persia and Michael, the archangel. We find the words of the angel to Daniel concerning his prayer.

Daniel 10:12

"...thy words were heard, and I am come for thy words."

Hallelujah! What a powerful scripture! The angel responds and says the minute heaven heard your prayer, I was dispatched simply by your words. The words that we speak in faith are heard and causes all of Heaven to move swiftly on our behalf for that which we speak.

We are never more like God than when we are creating with words. So create your world of Success and Prosperity by speaking it in faith. So I encourage you to build your world with words of faith. Everything seen exists because someone brought it from the unseen with words. Yes, even empires, companies, and successful ideas all began with words. Someone said it before we ever saw it.

BUILD YOUR WORLD WITH WORDS OF FAITH!

According to God's Word, you can have what you say. So, saying the right words can produce your desires or that which you believe in your heart. Whether good or bad, the words you say will reward you accordingly. Your words can testify for you or against you.

In Numbers 14, we see the account of the children of Israel who murmured and complained. They were constantly saying that they would die in the wilderness. This continual negativity redirected their destiny. God brought them out that He might take them in. But their words testified against them. God heard their words and fulfilled their words as they had believed in their hearts and spoken with their mouths.

Numbers 14:28

> *"...as surely as I live, saith the Lord, as ye have spoken in Mine ears, so will I do to you."*

Now the opposite is true of Joshua and Caleb. They spoke words of conquest and victory and as they spoke, they received. While everyone else doubted and spoke words to affirm their negative belief, Joshua and Caleb affirmed their belief with words of faith which reproduced after their own kind.

Numbers 13:30

> *"...Let us go up at once, and possess it; for we are well able to overcome it."*

So as you have received the vision for your success and prosperity, as you have pictured it ... now frame it with words. It has been said that a picture without a frame is not as valuable as a picture with a frame.

FRAME YOUR WORLD OF SUCCESS AND PROSPERITY WITH WORDS FILLED WITH FAITH!

(For additional scriptures to help in the "framing" process, see the Chapter on Successful Meditations.)

CHAPTER 8

Successful Meditations

"The law thou hast in writing must govern every utterance of thine mouth (Knox Trans.); recite it muse over it, keep it in your thoughts day and night; be careful to comply with what is written in it; for then thou shalt make thy way prosperous and then thou shalt have good success." **Joshua 1:8**

> **Meditation** – the act of reflecting upon; to engage in contemplation.

Meditation should play a very important part in the life of the Christian. We have shunned this important discipline primarily because it is practiced by eastern religions and the new age movement whose focus of worship and meditation is anyone but Jesus Christ.

Throughout scripture we are told to meditate. The reference to Christians as sheep is constant throughout the scriptures. In understanding sheep, you understand that sheep do not digest their food the way that humans do. Sheep ruminate. When sheep eat their food, it doesn't go immediately into the stomach to be digested, but it is constantly being brought back up and chewed upon until it is processed thoroughly. Ruminate means to chew cud. It also means to meditate. So you see, meditation is a normal process for the sheep of God.

I encourage you to meditate upon the following scriptures listed in this chapter. For further enrichment and enjoyment, look for the accompanying audio version of "Successful Meditations." This is a recording project mixed with scripture and music reinforcing Success and Prosperity.

II Chronicles 20:20

"Believe in the Lord your God, so shall ye be established; believe his prophets, so shall ye prosper."

Job 36:11

"If they obey and serve Him, they shall spend their days in prosperity, and their years in pleasures."

Psalm 1:1-3

"Blessed is the man that walketh not in the counsel of the ungodly, nor standeth in the way of sinners, nor sitteth in the seat of the scornful. But his delight is in the law of the Lord; and in His law doth he meditate day and night. And he shall be like a tree planted by the rivers of water, that bringeth forth its fruit in season; its leaf also shall not wither, and whatsoever he doeth shall prosper."

Proverbs 16:3

"Commit thy works unto the Lord, and thy thoughts shall be established."

Proverbs 22:29

"Seest thou a man diligent in his business? He shall stand before kings; he shall not stand before mere men."

Proverbs 8:12-21

"I Wisdom dwell with prudence, and find out knowledge of witty inventions. The fear of the Lord is to

hate evil; pride, and arrogancy, and the evil way, and the froward mouth, do I hate. Counsel is mine,

and sound wisdom: I am understanding; I have strength. By me kings reign, and princes decree justice. By me princes rule, and nobles, even all the judges of the earth. I love them that love me; and those that seek me early shall find me. Riches and honor are with me; yea, durable riches and righteousness. My fruit is better than gold, yea than fine gold; and my revenue than choice silver. I lead in the way of righteousness, in the midst of the paths of judgment: That I may cause those that love me to inherit substance: and I will fill their treasures."

Isaiah 48:17b (NIV)

"This is what the Lord says, your redeemer, the Holy One of Israel, I am the Lord your God, who teaches You what is best for you, who directs you in the way You should go."

Isaiah 41:10

"Fear thou not; for I am with thee: be not dismayed; for I am thy God: I will strengthen thee; yea, I will help thee; yea, I will uphold thee with the right hand of My righteousness."

Isaiah 45:2-3

"I will go before thee, and make the crooked places

straight: I will break in pieces the gates of brass, and cut in sunder the bars of iron: And I will give thee the treasures of darkness, and hidden riches of secret places, that thou mayest know that I, the Lord which call thee by thy name and the God of Israel."

3 John 2

"Beloved, I wish above all things that thou mayest prosper and be in health, even as thy soul prospereth."

Philemon 6

"That the communication of thy faith may become effectual by the acknowledging of every good thing which is in you in Christ Jesus."

Psalm 37:4

"Delight yourself in the Lord and He will give you the desires of your heart."

Proverbs 10:4 (NIV)

"Lazy hands make a man poor, but the diligent hands bring wealth."

Proverbs 10:24 (NIV)

"What the wicked dreads, will overtake him; what the righteous desire will be granted."

2 Corinthians 8:9

"For ye know the grace of our Lord Jesus Christ, that though He was rich, yet for your sakes He became poor, that ye through His poverty might be rich."

Philippians 4:6

"Be careful for nothing; but in everthing by prayer and supplication with thanksgiving let your requests be made known unto God."

John 10:10

"The thief cometh not, but for to steal, and to kill, and to destroy: I am come that they might have life, and that they might have it more abundantly."

Meditating empowers your subconscious mind as discussed in Chapter 4. The continual positive reinforcement of these scriptures will transform your mind as directed in Romans 12:2. The transformation of the mind directly affects the heart thus teaching your mouth (Proverbs 16:23) what your heart and mind believes. The Word declares that everything must be established by two or three witnesses. Our mind, heart, and our mouths are now in agreement. Agreement is now established … it is fixed. Success is inevitable!

Additional Scriptures for Mediation:

Deuteronomy 31:6-8; Psalm 35:27(b); Proverbs 3:5; Philippians 4:19; Hebrews 10:35; Habbakuk 2:4; Psalm 27:1; 2 Timothy 1:7; Psalm 56:11; Isaiah 51:7; Psalm 37:23; Psalm 84:11(b); Psalm 92:12; Isaiah 55:11.

CHAPTER 9

Praying For Success

As we strive to become all that God has intended for us to become, it must be reinforced by prayer. Otherwise it is very possible to pursue the wrong thing and call it success.

Therefore, we must pray according to God's will for our lives. Praying in this manner can be seen in the model of prayer, where we are taught to pray:

> "Thy Kingdom come, Thy will be done in earth as it is in heaven."

To exhibit true success, we must succeed at what God has already designed and destined for our lives. Prayer can line us up with the purposes of God. Anything less than what God has already designed for us is a lessor purpose. To truly experience biblical success, we must succeed in the greater purposes of God for our lives. Prayer not only reveals these purposes, but it keeps the communication line open with the designer of your dreams and visions.

I AM ONLY SUCCESSFUL WHEN I DO WHAT I WAS CREATED AND ASSIGNED TO DO!

The biblical account of the search for Isaac's bride is a beautiful illustration of success. The chief servant of Abraham was given the assignment of finding a wife for Isaac. But this assignment came with specifications.

Genesis 24:3-4 (NKJV)

"...you will not take a wife for my son from the daughters of the Canaanites, among whom I dwell; but you shall go to my country and to my family, and take a wife for my son Isaac."

Note the specifics of the assignment. The servant was very interested in succeeding. So much so that he asked questions for clarity.

Genesis 24:5-6,8 (NKJV)

"And the servant said to him, perhaps the woman will not be willing to follow me to this land. Must I take your son back to the land from which you came? But Abraham said to him, Beware that you do not take my son back there....And if the woman is not willing to follow you, then you will be released from this oath; only do not take my son back there."

After receiving instructions, the servant prepared himself for the assignment and set out to do what he had been assigned to.

In reading this story you will find where the servant literally prayed that he would succeed. How often do we pray for success? Often we pray for permission to do something, but rarely do we pray that we would succeed in doing it. Christians often pray to discern if we should attempt something. But his prayer was to succeed in his assignment.

Genesis 24:12-15

"...O Lord God of my master Abraham, please

give me success this day, and show kindness to my master Abraham. Behold, here I stand by the well of water, and the daughters of the men of the city are coming out to draw water. Now let it be that the young woman to whom I say, please let down your pitcher that I may drink and she says drink, and I will also give your camels a drink; let her be the one you have appointed for your servant Isaac. And by this I will know that you have shown kindness to my master. And it happened, before he had finished speaking ....."

The conclusion of the matter is that the servant found a bride for Isaac according to the instructions and specifications given. Prayer according to the Word of God is according to the specifications given. Coupled with what you believe God has spoken to you concerning your dreams, vision, or assignment, you should pray the scriptures given in the previous chapter, Successful Mediations. Prayer according to God's Word is PROSPEROUS! That means, it brings what is profitable!

The servant of Abraham prayed into existence how his assignment was to be fulfilled. Learn to pray your assignment. You are assigned to...

SUCCEED AND PROSPER!

Praying is saying! Say what you are assigned to do and become. Pray in accordance with God's will and God's Word. It is God's will and God's Word for you to **SUCCEED AND PROSPER!**

Pray prophetically! Praying prophetically is speaking the words or promises of God to create God's realities. We are constantly reminded of the great and precious promises that we have as New Testament believers. Yet, we choose not to live our lives by promises but rather live them by facts substantiated by the visible. But I say, live by promises. They have eternal value. My Executive and Editorial Assistant is always talking about spending promises. You can spend promises when you don't have money.

When you think of the word 'PROMISE', think…

Prophetic

Release

Of the

Mind of God

Inspired by

Scripture which is

Empowered

Seed!

CHAPTER 10

S_CCESS What's Missing?

Deuteronomy 8:18

"For it is He that giveth thee power to get wealth, that He may establish His covenant which He sware unto thy fathers, as is this day."

God has given us every tool to Prosper. He has given us seed, so that we can sow. For the scripture teaches, **He giveth seed to the sower. (Isaiah 55:10)** Many Christians have a wilderness mentality concerning provisions and prosperity. What they say is that they are waiting on God. I say "God is waiting on you."

The following statement is not meant to put down anyone. Many Christians are waiting on God like those persons who may receive welfare or any other assistance. These persons are waiting on their provisions.

(You) Make Your Way Prosperous

It is time for welfare reform! Haven't you noticed that even in the natural, our country has made an aggressive move towards reforming the welfare system. So must we be about reform in the church. The wilderness mentality waits for manna and quail. But God has ceased raining manna and is now raining seed for you to sow. What seed?

Do you know what manna was? Manna was a food eaten by the Israelites during their travels in the wilderness. It was white and flaky and looked like small _**seeds**_. Seeds. Manna was seed. I believe this seed was God's preparation to them to enter into their Promised Land. No longer would they have to simply rely on the seed falling down from heaven, but in Canaan, they could plant seed that grows up to God. This seed after it came down, would then be gathered, ground and baked in pans to make cakes. **(Numbers 11:8)**

Proverbs 12:11

"He who tills his land will be satisfied with bread, but he who follows frivolity is devoid of understanding."

I believe that God is still giving seed. But this seed must be planted, harvested and turned into bread for us. **Isaiah 55:10(b)** states that the seed is watered and produces more seed and bread to the eater. So let's take the seed that God gives us to produce our own harvest. We must give ourselves without slack to the seed given to us from God. In so doing, we are watering and nurturing the seed that will bring forth a bountiful harvest.

The seed I'm talking about is that idea or thought which God has put in your heart that will bring you a harvest. I believe that God is constantly giving us seed in the form of ideas. Once planted or acted upon, these ideas produce more ideas and a harvest for us to partake of. After all, the Bible teaches that we should be the first partakers of our fruit. So take the God idea (the seed) and produce a harvest.

It seems to me that responsibility is quite evasive in the Christian community. Everybody wants the privileges of Kingdom citizenship, but few want to take the responsibility of taking their inheritance or lot in life. Responsibility is an act of the will. The Word of God declares in **Isaiah 1:19:**

> *"If ye be willing and obedient, ye shall eat the good of the land."*

Prosperity demands responsibility. The Bible is clear concerning our role in our own prosperity and wealth. Diligence comes as a result of our having made a decision to do something. The key word is the decision to DO! If we are diligent, God assures us good results.

Proverbs 10:4

> *"he becometh poor that dealeth with a slack hand: but the hand of the diligent maketh rich."*

So make certain that you do not become slack in doing your part for God is not slack concerning his promises towards you.

"NEVER GIVE UP, LET UP, OR SHUT UP TILL GOD TAKES YOU UP!"
Peter Daniels

Like the children of Israel, and as spiritual Israel, God has delivered us from bondage. He has brought us out. He has brought us out to take us in! Glory to God. Don't settle for being free. Be free to Succeed and Prosper. Freedom is not enough for persons who are truly free. They also desire the freedom to expand and be all that they can be. "Be all that you can be" really ought to be offered by God's church. However, the church who is not 'Kingdom' minded is not interested in personal growth and development. The Gospel of the Kingdom must be preached to really motivate and encourage God's people to be all that they were designed and destined to be. Jesus declared that the Gospel of the Kingdom must be preached. The Gospel of the Kingdom includes Success and Prosperity.

CHAPTER 11

It's Not a Sin To Prosper

"Fear not, little flock; for it is your Father's good pleasure to give you the kingdom." **(Luke 12:32)**

Wealth - Much money or property; riches; resources; a large quantity; abundance.

Poverty - Condition of being poor: lacking what is needed; poor quality.

PROSPER – to be successful; have good fortune; thrive; flourish.

When we really understand who we are in Christ and the inheritance that we have because of who we are, our perspective of Prosperity and Success will change drastically. It is God's pleasure to prosper all of those who are his servants. If you are one of those persons, then you have God's approval to be prosperous.

Psalm 35:27

"Let them shout for joy, and be glad, that favor my righteous cause: yea, let them say continually, Let the Lord be magnified, which hath pleasure in the prosperity of His servant."

Success and Prosperity have more to do with self-worth than networth. Self worth determines net worth. You see, once I know that God has made me extremely valuable and that God's wealth for God's people is inside of God's people, then I see myself as valuable. Recognizing this value, my net worth increases immediately. The beginning of increase is the realization of self worth.

WEALTH AND PROSPERITY

Wealth and Prosperity are major topics in the scripture. But few messages are ever preached or taught. Yet, much time is spent in most churches literally "begging" for money that people don't really have. Why? Because most Christians live beneath their economic potential. One of the most annoying things to me personally is to sit through a time during some services called the offering. Manipulation, witchcraft, and sometimes even lying are all used to try and get something called money. Money is a product of wealth and prosperity.

It is therefore my firm belief that equal energies need to be given to people causing them to believe that it really is God's idea for them to prosper.

3 John 2

"Beloved, I wish above all things that you prosper and be in good health even as your soul prospers."

Wealth has been so misunderstood that the mention of it causes one to focus only on what it can bring. Wealth is not money, but it produces money. While many love to focus in on the negative trappings of the wealthy, we fail to acknowledge the benefits of wealth. Simply because a person does not rightly prioritize money in his/her life doesn't make money evil. Money is not evil! The love of money is what God calls evil.

1 Timothy 6:1

"For the love of money is a root of all kinds of evil."

Notice that the scriptures say that the love of money is "**A**" root not specifically "**THE**" root. There are several roots that evil grows from. Two of those roots are poverty and lack! Much of the evil manifested in our society by both Christians and non-Christians stem from poverty and lack. Non-Christians and Christians steal in an attempt to meet needs caused by poverty and lack. While non-Christians may commit theft in other forms, Christians rob God (See Malachi) by not tithing. God calls this thievery. This is evil.

What are other evils that come from poverty and lack? Jealousy. When we don't have or can't have something that we desire and see other people with it, then we become envious and jealous. This is evil! When we desire something that someone else has and have not the means or faith to acquire it, then covetousness enters in. This is evil! When persons don't have what they desire, strife is manifested. This is evil! Getting to this root of evil includes experiencing success and prosperity.

As Christians we need to check our root system. The righteous flourish when they are planted by rivers of living water and in the courts of the Lord. Always remember ... The fruit is exactly like the root!

Proverbs 12:12 (NKJV)

"The wicked covet the catch of evil men, but the root of the righteous yields fruit."

With the understanding that wealth and prosperity can not be confined to money, we can see that wealth and prosperity is God's idea not the devil's. Remember ... it was God's idea for his creation to be fruitful, multiply, increase and abound. Genesis is the seedbed for wealth and prosperity. As New Testament Christians, we constantly refer to the Abrahamic Covenant. This covenant is established on the Promises of God given in Genesis 12.

Genesis 12:1-3 (NKJV)

"Now the Lord had said to Abram: Get thee out of your country, from your family and from your father's house, to a land that I will show you. I will make you a great nation; I will bless you and make your name great; and you shall be a blessing. I will bless those who bless you, and curse him who curses you; and in you all the families of the earth shall be blessed."

GET OUT OF UR, THE PLACE OF FAMILIARITY AND COMFORT!

But God desired even more. Hebrews 8:6 declares that a better covenant with better promises has been established because of Jesus Christ. Hallelujah!

"But now hath He obtained a more excellent ministry, by how much also He is the mediator of a better covenant established upon better promises."

So as you see, God's heart is to PROSPER his people. The Bible is replete with prosperous people: Adam, Abraham, Isaac, Jacob, Joseph, The Nation of Israel when coming out of Egypt, Job, David, Solomon, Joseph of Arimathea, and the list goes on.

I find it interesting that Abram's tithe to Melchizedek appears only after Abram has something to tithe from. God's will is that each of us would live a life filled with abundance, an OVERFLOWING life.

CHAPTER 12

Creating an Overflow

Most Christians are so "sacrifice" minded, that they have depleted themselves and their resources. This mentality has produced angry, bitter, and frustrated Christians. There are times that God's demands sacrifice. But God created you and filled you with Himself. Having done so, you have been filled beyond that which you have the capacity to contain.

When we DARE to Succeed and Prosper, we are conscious that others are depending on our success. Success leaves something for generations to come. As we study the lives of most of the Patriarchs, we are impacted by their great level of Success and Prosperity. These saints of the Old Testament have no advantage over us.

Romans 8:32

"He that spared not His own Son, but delivered Him up for us all, how shall he not with Him also freely give us all things?"

God's call to his people for Success and Prosperity is not just for us. However, it is for us to perpetuate the covenant or establish God's covenant in the earth and also to create an OVERFLOW!

Abraham succeeded and left an inheritance and covenant for all that would believe on his God including those who were afar off. Isaac continued in his father's legacy of faith leaving a blessing for his son, Jacob. Jacob worked for his uncle and greatly increased Laban's flocks and herds. Jacobs creativity and personal efforts supported by God's blessings created so much, that he increased his own flocks and had great wealth to take with him when he left. Jacob succeeded by supplying the twelve-(12) tribes of Israel and fostering Joseph's dream of dominion. Joseph succeeded in Potiphar's House and Potiphar prospered. Joseph succeeded in prison and the warden and others imprisoned fared well. Remember the butler. **(Genesis 40:21)** Joseph succeeded and prospered in Pharaoh's palace and all of Egypt lived. Success and Prosperity is for you, and those around, and after you. Moses succeeded in leading the children of Israel out of bondage. Israel not only gained freedom, but they gained great wealth in the process. Joshua succeeded at leading the children of Israel into their Promised Land and into their inheritance. Joshua's success as promised in Joshua 1:8 provided land beyond their imagination and everything that their inherited land could produce.

As we conclude this review of God's successful and prosperous people let us go back to David. David's success in defeating Goliath brought the nation of Israel victory over all the Philistines.

1 Samuel 17:51

"Therefore David ran and stood over the Philistine, took his sword and drew it out of its sheath and killed him, and cut off his head with it. And when the Philistines saw that their champion was dead, they fled."

One man's successful DARE gave the entire army of Israel courage to pursue and conquer. For the Bible says that they not only defeated them, but the children of Israel plundered their tents. **(1 Sam 17:53)** This means that not only did they win the battle, but also they took the possessions of the Phillistines back home with them. They had what they already owned back at home, but they increased because of David's DARE To Succeed and Prosper! Who is waiting on you to Succeed and Prosper?

If we continue reading on, we find that this was simply the beginning of Success and Prosperity for David and Israel under David's leadership. David knew the Lord had established him or raised him up to be King over Israel. This was done not for David to brag about how successful he had been, but for the sake of His people Israel.

2 Samuel 5:12

"And David perceived that the Lord had established him king over Israel, and that He had exalted his kingdom for His people's sake."

There are many people who desire such personal success, but few who achieve it. Statistics show that only five percent (5%) do so. This 5% generates the surplus or the overflow in our society that makes it rich enough to support the less capable; and give a good life to all that will work to achieve it. While some would think it honorable to be in this small minority of 5%, God has made it possible for all who would DARE to Succeed and Prosper, creating an overflow for their families, generations, and churches.

Creating a surplus, an abundance, an Overflow is the result of Success. This surplus is to meet needs (personal and others). In **Matthew 6:19**, we find this famous quote of Jesus:

> *"Do not lay up for yourselves treasures on earth ... but lay up for yourselves treasures in heaven..."*

This scripture deals with stockpiling or hoarding resources not acquiring them. For even Jesus found no problem with gaining or acquiring more.

Note that the scripture teaches "lay not up for yourselves..." The stockpiling or hoarding of treasures should not be for ourselves, lest we misinterpret the purpose for wealth. Remember, wealth is to perpetuate the covenant. To draw others into the Kingdom of God. So never mistake God"'s words concerning wealth and prosperity as Him not wanting you to have wealth. Just make certain that wealth doesn't have you. You can have anything, but possess nothing!

In **Matthew 25:14-30** we find another one of Jesus' discussions concerning money.

> *"For the Kingdom of Heaven is a man travelling into a far country, who called his own servants, and delivered unto them his goods. And unto one he gave five talents, to another two, and to another one; to*

every man according to his several ability; and straightway took his journey. Then he that had received the five talents went and traded with the same, and made them other five talents. And likewise he that had received two, he also gained other two. But he that had received one went and digged in the earth, and hid his lord's money. After a long time, the Lord of those servants cometh, and reckoned with them. And so he that had received five talents came and brought other five talents, saying, Lord, thou delivered unto me five talents: behold, I have gained beside them five talents more. His lord said unto Him, Well done, thou good and faithful servant: thou hast been faithful over a few things, I will make thee ruler over many things: enter thou into the joy of thy lord. He also that had received two talents came and said, lord, thou deliveredst unto me two talents: behold I have gained two other talents beside them. His lord said unto him, well done, good and faithful servant; thou hast been faithful over a few things, I will make thee ruler over many things: enter thou into the joy of thy lord. Then he which had received the one talent came and said, lord, I knew thee that thou art an hard man, reaping where thou hast not sown, and gathering where thou hast not strawed: and I was afraid, and went and hid thy talent in the earth: lo, there thou hast that is thine. His lord answered and said unto him, thou wicked and slothful servant, thou knewest that I reap where I sowed not, and gather where I have not strawed: thou oughtest therefore to have put my money to the exchangers, and then at my coming I should have received mine own with usury. Take therefore the talent from him, and give it unto him which hath ten talents. For unto every one that hath shall be given, and he shall have abundance: but from him that hath not shall be taken away even that which he hath. And cast ye unprofitable servant into outer darkness: There shall be weeping and gnashing of teeth."

To Succeed and Prosper signals that you can be trusted with more. When one succeeds on a job, he can then be given more responsibilities or a different assignment due to his/her success and fruitfulness. The world is filled with people who bear witness to the benefits of succeeding.

It is time that the people of God, those called by His name, accept the challenges of the giants of their lives with the assurance of victory because of God's promises and covenant. We can do so because we have the assurance of victory because of God's promises, God's covenant, and our faith.

<u>1 John 5:4</u>

"For whatever is born of God overcomes the world. and this is the victory that has overcome the world – even our faith."

With this assurance of victory, you should **DARE TO:**

- ✓ Live in Your Promised land of Wealth and Abundance!

- ✓ Think what God thinks toward you and DREAM BIG!

- ✓ Get rid of your Losing Mentality!

- ✓ Walk in Boldness, Courage, Faith and Victory!

- ✓ Be Knowledgeable of and Zealous for God's plan for your life!

- ✓ Activate your Ideas and Imagination to Create a fortune to meet needs of God's people everywhere!

- ✓ Speak What You Believe!

- ✓ See Yourself as God Sees You by Filling Your Subconscious with dreams and imaginations!

Dare To Succeed and Prosper

- ✓ Walk out of Fear and into Faith To Be Bold as a Lion!

- ✓ Write out and Pray your assignment, goals, dreams, or vision!

- ✓ Empower your consciousness with Joy, Peace, Love, Assurance, Courage, and a sense of Accomplishment.

- ✓ Know Your Self-worth and Increase Your Net Worth

- ✓ Get rid of your settling mentality and read materials that will help you succeed!

- ✓ Believe beyond your past/present and into your Future!

- ✓ Surround yourself with success-oriented people!

- ✓ Come out of your religious mindset and …

- ✓ **<u>SUCCEED AND PROSPER</u>**!

Apostle Bennie Fluellen

Appendix 1

All Scriptures used in this book.

Ephesians 2:10

John 17:4

II Timothy 4:7

Joshua 1:5-9

Matthew 11:12

I Samuel 17:1-8

Deuteronomy 31:8

Psalm 27:1

Isaiah 41:10

Romans 8:15a

II Timothy 1:7

Matthew 25:24-27

Joshua 1:6

Joshua 1:7

Joshua 1:9

I Samuel 17:16

I Samuel 17:25

Proverbs 28:1

Philemon 3:6

Romans 12:11

Titus 2:14

I Samuel 17:29

John 10:10

Deuteronomy 31:6-8

Psalm 35:27b

Proverbs 3:5

Philippians 4:19

Hebrews 10:35

Habbakuk 2:4

Psalm 27:1

II Timothy 1:7

Psalm 56:11

Isaiah 51:7

Psalm 37:23

Apostle Bennie Fluellen

Psalm 84:11b

Psalm 92:12

Isaiah 55:11

Romans 12:2

Proverbs 28:1

Philemon 3:6

Romans 12:11

Titus 2:14

I Samuel 17:29

John 10:10

Romans 12:2

Proverbs 23:7

Psalm 27:1-14

Ephesians 3:20

Proverbs 29:18

Habbakuk 2:1-4

I Corinthians 2:9-12

Joshua 1:8b

Matthew 6:33

Dare To Succeed and Prosper

Habbakuk 2:4

Hebrews 10:38

Psalm 1:1-3

Joshua 1:8

Hebrews 11:3

Psalm 19:14

Matthew 12:34-37

Genesis 1:3

Genesis 1:6

Genesis 1:9

Genesis 1:11

Genesis 1:14-15

Genesis 1:20

Genesis 1:22

Genesis 1:24

Genesis 1:26

Genesis 1:28

Romans 14:23

James 2:14; 17-18

Apostle Bennie Fluellen

Psalm 116:10

Romans 10:10

Proverbs 16:23

Mark 11:22-24

Daniel 9:3-19

Daniel 10:12

Numbers 14:28

Numbers 13:30

II Chronicles 20:20

Job 36:11

Psalm 1:1-3

Proverbs 16:3

Proverbs 22:29

Proverbs 8:12-21

Isaiah 41:10

Isaiah 45:2-3

III John 2

Philemon 6

Psalm 37:4

Proverbs 10:4

Proverbs 10:24

II Corinthians 8:9

Philippians 4:6

John 10:10

Romans 12:2

Proverbs 16:23

Genesis 24:3-4

Genesis 24:5-6; 8

Genesis 24: 12-15

Deuteronomy 8:18

Isaiah 55:10

Numbers 11:8

Proverbs 12:11

Isaiah 55:10b

Isaiah 1:19

Proverbs 10:4

Luke 12:32

Psalm 35:27

III John 2

I Timothy 6:1

Proverbs 12:12

Genesis 12:1-3

Hebrews 8:6

Romans 8:32

Genesis 40:21

I Samuel 17:51

I Samuel 17:53

II Samuel 5:12

Matthew 6:19

Matthew 25:14

I John 5:4

Appendix 2

Write out your vision or idea(s) that God has given you.

Write the Vision, Make it Plain!

Apostle Bennie Fluellen

Think On These Things

➢ "To be Successful and Prosperous, You Must Have A 'Be' attitude."   *Apostle Bennie Fluellen*

➢ "Success Is Your Birthright"   *Alan Cohen*

➢ "The People in my life and my life experiences are key to my Success and Prosperity."

Apostle Bennie Fluellen

➢ "Do What You Came here to Do!" *Alan Cohen*

➢ "To See Yourself as a Success, You Must Change Your View. You Must See Yourself as God Sees You."   *Pastor Bennie Fluellen*

➢ "Think You can, or think you can't, and either way you'll be correct."   *Henry Ford*

SOWING

AND

REAPING

Apostle Bennie Fluellen

Sow A Thought,

Reap A Word;

Sow a Word,

Reap a Deed;

Sow a Deed,

Reap a Habit;

Sow a Habit,

Reap a Character;

Sow A Character,

Reap a Destiny!

ABOUT THE AUTHOR

Believer ... Husband ... Father ... Apostle ... Teacher ... Songwriter ... Recording Artist ... Worshipper ... Worship Leader... Author.... And Entrepreneur!

Apostle Bennie Fluellen is the Overseer and Apostle to Overflow Ministries Covenant Church, whose mission rests upon *"Building the Foundation of Family, Marriage, Relationships, Performing Arts & Entrepreneurs'."* Covenant is the hallmark of Overflow Ministries. Apostle Bennie is the founder and spiritual father to the spiritual son's involved in Covenant Family Fellowship of Churches; a group of pastors and local churches who desire to relate to and experience the new testament paradigm of church. He serves the members of CFFC by assisting, fathering, mentoring, and guiding other Senior Pastors in the work of their respective local church.

Before founding Overflow Ministries Covenant Church, Apostle Bennie served as Assistant Pastor of Christ Emmanuel Christian Fellowship, Cincinnati, Ohio for more than fifteen years serving faithfully the vision of Bishop Michael E. Dantley. He served as visionary and leader with oversight of Congregational Life, Kingdom Life, Administration, Operations, and Finance, and all of the entrepreneurial and economic ventures of the ministry. As an avid worshipper, Apostle Bennie specifically served in the area of Worship & Arts as choir director, worship leader, and lead vocalist during those years.

Apostle Bennie Fluellen

Apostle Bennie (affectionately called and known as "Pop", "Dad" or "My Apostle") is known for his passionate worship and leading others in unforgettable, prophetic worship experiences. His earth shaking teachings on topics such as: the New Testament Church, Church Government, Healing the Soul, Worship, and Relationships to name a few, literally dismantles the religious and traditional systems within the Body of Christ. The explosive teaching, preaching and singing ministry of Apostle Bennie Fluellen continues to bless and equip the Body of Christ. His outspoken messages have shaken the gates of hell, liberating the captive bound into an overflowing life of true relationship with Christ Jesus.

His other published works include *D.A.R.E. to Succeed and Prosper* - putting the pen to what he has experienced with the wisdom and understanding of how to pragmatically help people succeed; Successful Meditations, a music and word CD utilized in churches, businesses, hospitals, etc. to help bring healing and right thinking to people, Life In Context, and Life In High Definition. As founder of *Coat of Color Ministries, Inc., a* ministry where he equips the saints outside of Overflow Ministries Covenant Church and where he imparts apostolically to the Body of Christ nationally and internationally. Apostle is impacting the Body of Christ with revelatory teaching and preaching establishing God's order for the New Testament Church. He also serves the marketplace in business, corporate, and educational arenas as a certified trainer in the area of diversity and interpersonal relationship skills.

Apostle Bennie can be seen and heard on regional television and radio stations and can be heard on, "Successful Meditations", and "Worship, My Highest Call" as songwriter, lead vocalist, and Executive Producer. These music projects accompany his books, "D.A.R.E. To Succeed and Prosper." And "Worship, My Highest Call". You will also find Apostle Bennie on the Nation of Praise project (Heirs Media Group), where he is the writer and lead vocalist of the song "Healing In His Wings". His latest endeavor, "Worship…My Highest Call," released March 2010 along with a devotional booklet entitled the same was nominated 2010 Gospel Music People's Choice "Praise and Worship CD of the Year", "Male Lead Vocalist of the Year", "Gospel CD of The Year".

As a teaching and building apostle, he travels extensively building foundations in the areas of church leadership and government and worship. He is a sought after Man of God in the area of music and worship creating prophetic and supernatural spiritual environments through "Worship Experiences, intentionally designed services for people to encounter God through music and worship.

To contact or schedule Apostle Bennie for any of your events, please call Anitra Fluellen-Scott at 513-742-3569.

www.ingramcontent.com/pod-product-compliance
Lightning Source LLC
Chambersburg PA
CBHW071148090426
42736CB00012B/2270